NORTHERN

AND PROUD OF IT

CARI ROSEN

summersdale

NORTHERN AND PROUD OF IT

Summersdale Publishers Ltd
46 West Street
Chichester
West Sussex
PO19 1RP
UK

www.summersdale.com

Printed and bound in the Czech Republic

ISBN: 978-1-84953-684-4

Substantial discounts on bulk quantities of Summersdale books are available to corporations, professional associations and other organisations. For details contact Nicky Douglas by telephone: +44 (0) 1243 756902, fax: +44 (0) 1243 786300 or email: nicky@summersdale.com.

CONTENTS

INTRODUCTION

They say it's grim up north – but they're wrong. Yes, it rains a lot (especially in Manchester) and it can get a bit nippy but, actually, it's great up north and there are many (many) reasons why. Whether it's culture, countryside or *Coronation Street* you're after, we've got plenty to offer.

Northern England is home to the most beautiful landscape, the friendliest people, the tastiest food and so much more. The slightest hint of bias creeping in, perhaps, but then there are so many things for us to celebrate. Join us on a journey through the land of Yorkshire pud, Victoria Wood, the Brontës and the Beatles, and discover why we will always be Northern… and proud of it.

MAKING HISTORY

HISTORY

IMPORTANT DATES
IN OUR HISTORY

The first recorded Mersey ferry sailed as far back as **1150**. And to think it only took Gerry and the Pacemakers another 815 years to write a song about it. The Benedictine monks, who ran (or rather rowed) the service, were even granted a Royal Charter by Edward III in **1330**. The ferries still run today. Although without oars. Or monks.

On the theme of transport, the world's first locomotive-hauled passenger service opened in **1825**, running between Stockton and Darlington. Thanks for this go in no small part to Northumberland-born George Stephenson (later dubbed 'Father of the Railways') and his son Robert, who together also invented the famous Stephenson's *Rocket*. A man of many talents, and a stickler when it came to salads, George's other inventions included the cucumber straightener.

Dark and true and tender is the North.

ALFRED, LORD TENNYSON

It's been featured in countless movies, and is probably the most famous park on the planet. But how many visitors to New York's Central Park are aware that the inspiration behind it came from… the Wirral? Birkenhead Park – widely acknowledged to be the UK's first municipal park – was opened on **5 April 1847**. Frederick Law Olmsted, an American landscape architect who visited the area three years later, rued the fact that America had 'nothing to be thought of as comparable with this People's Garden' and got to work. Central Park opened to the public seven years later.

In **1928** Harry Ramsden opened his first fish and chip shop in Guiseley, Leeds, thus laying the foundations for what's become Britain's longest established chain of restaurants. According to the National Federation of Fish Friers (who knew?), Harry Ramsden's Bournemouth restaurant is the largest chippie in the UK with 417 covers. But as that's down south, let us visit instead the longest running chippie still in operation (in Yeadon, Leeds), which has been frying continuously since **1865**.

A free health service available to all, regardless of class, wealth or income: where would we be without the NHS? Founded in Manchester in **July 1948** by Health Minister Aneurin 'Nye' Bevan, it is now the largest publicly funded health service in the world. Around 1 in 23 people in England and Wales work for the NHS, making it one of the biggest employers in the world (some of the others being the Indian Railways, the Walmart chain and the Chinese People's Liberation Army).

This island is made mainly
of coal and surrounded by
fish. Only an organising
genius could produce
a shortage of coal and
fish at the same time.

ANEURIN BEVAN

Premium Bonds were launched on Budget Day 1956 – and the first draw took place on **1 June 1957** in Lytham St Annes, Lancashire. Since then ERNIE – the Electronic Random Number Indicator Equipment (rather than the man who drove the fastest milk float in the West) has generated the winning numbers for more than £15 billion worth of prizes. The odds of each £1 bond winning a prize are 26,000 : 1. Probably not worth giving up the day job…

People in
Liverpool don't
move very far,
you know.

RINGO STARR

The most significant date in all of
TV history (we may be biased here)
is **9 December 1960,** when the very
first episode of *Coronation Street* was
broadcast to the nation. Originally named
Florizel Street (which was changed when
someone mentioned it sounded more
like a disinfectant than a soap), it's been
a mainstay of the TV schedules since the
start – and over half a century later, locals
are still gathering in the Rovers Return for
half a bitter and a nice plate of hotpot.

I think life without *Coronation Street* would be unthinkable. It's part of all our lives.

MICHAEL PARKINSON

The Beatles played their first concert at Liverpool's Cavern Club at lunchtime on **9 February 1961**. The performance, which wasn't advertised, earned the group a total of £5 – although George Harrison was lucky to get his cut after turning up in jeans, which were banned by the club. A bouncer finally took pity on him and let him in. Harrison was rumoured to like Jelly Babies: at later gigs the band would be pelted with confectionery by eager fans, although he did beg them to stop after being hit in the eye by a boiled sweet.

On **29 May 1968** Manchester United became the first English club to win the European Cup when they beat Benfica 4–1 at Wembley after extra time. In the 58-year history of the competition to date, clubs from the North have lifted the trophy exactly double the number of times of clubs from the South. Just saying…

Louise Brown, the world's first 'test-tube baby' was born in Oldham and District General Hospital, Lancashire, on **25 July 1978**. Since then around five million IVF babies have been born in Britain, over half of them since 2007. Robert Edwards (Northern… from Batley, Yorkshire) – who along with Patrick Steptoe pioneered in vitro fertilisation – was awarded the Nobel Prize in Physiology or Medicine in 2010.

WE CAN BE HEROES

PEOPLE WE CAN BE PROUD TO CALL OUR OWN

They don't get much more heroic than **Emmeline Pankhurst**, who led the British suffragette movement to help win women the right to vote. Born in Manchester, she died in 1928, just weeks before the vote was finally extended to all women over the age of 21. In 1999 she was named one of the 100 most remarkable people of the twentieth century by *Time* magazine.

Generally speaking, its citizens have been liberal in their sentiments, defenders of free speech and liberty of opinion.

EMMELINE PANKHURST ON MANCHESTER

Another Mancunian, **Ethel 'Sunny' Lowry**, became the first British woman to swim the Channel in 1933. As part of her preparation she ate 40 eggs (mainly in omelettes) a week and ditched her traditional, heavy woollen swimsuit for a two-piece costume – considered so risqué for the times that some branded her a harlot for daring to bare her knees. Nonetheless, she was feted as a hero – and in her mid-nineties coached David Walliams before he attempted his own cross-Channel swim in 2006.

The first woman to fly solo from England to Australia was **Amy Johnson** in 1930. Born in Hull, she went on to break a number of other aviation records and was also awarded a CBE. At the hi-de-high point of her fame, she was invited to be guest of honour at the opening of the very first Butlins holiday camp in Skegness in 1936. Her statue stands in Prospect Street, Hull, to this day.

One of the best-loved and most successful double act in history, Morecambe and Wise (aka **Eric Morecambe** – born in Morecambe – and **Ernie Wise** – born in Bramley, Leeds) became a national institution and split the sides of their adoring public for decades: *The Morecambe & Wise Show* ran from 1968–77, but the reruns prove just as popular today and their Christmas specials remain one of the most important parts of any festive TV schedule.

I used to play football
when I was young but
then my eyes went bad –
so I became a referee.

ERIC MORECAMBE

Although most people identify **Robin Hood** – he of robbing-the-rich-to-pay-the-poor and Maid Marian fame – with Nottingham, legend has it that the heroic outlaw hailed, in fact, from the North. Or perhaps that should be legends plural, since there are hypotheses aplenty about who the archer extraordinaire really was. But the most popular theories suggest he came from somewhere in Yorkshire (the somewhere variously being York, Wakefield and a number of other towns in between).

As modern-day heroes go, they don't come much more popular (or indeed speedy) than Olympic heptathlon champion and poster girl of London 2012, **Jessica Ennis-Hill**: her time in the 100 metres hurdles was the fastest ever run in a heptathlon. Sheffield born and bred, she graduated from the city's university with a degree in psychology. She's been granted the Freedom of the City of Sheffield. Oh, and she supports Sheffield United. There's definitely a theme there…

England's greatest gardener also hails from the North: **Lancelot 'Capability' Brown** is probably the best-known landscape architect (or, as he described himself, 'place-maker') ever. Famed for the speed at which he worked, he transformed the grounds of stately homes including Chatsworth, Longleat and Blenheim Palace. From 1764 until his death in 1783, he was Chief Gardener at Hampton Court Palace. We can only guess how flattered he would have been by having a prog rock band named after him in the 1970s.

The 'incomparable' footballing brothers **Bobby and Jack Charlton** are Northern through and through. Born in Ashington, Northumberland, Bobby, one of the greatest midfielders of all time, remains one of Manchester United's all-time heroes. In the words of Sir Matt Busby, 'He was as near perfection as man and player as it is possible to be.' Jack managed Middlesbrough, Sheffield Wednesday and Newcastle United and, as a player, helped Leeds to their first ever Football League title. Oh, and together they won the World Cup in 1966 – the only British brothers ever to lift the Jules Rimet Trophy.

Prime Minister twice, but perhaps most famous for his reforms of criminal law and the prison service, **Robert Peel** created the Metropolitan Police Force (aka the Met) in 1829. He became known as the 'father of modern policing' – and policemen became known as 'bobbies' in his honour. There are at least 12 statues of Peel in locations across the UK, including one outside the Robert Peel pub in Bury.

The right honourable gentleman is reminiscent of a poker. The only difference is that a poker gives off the occasional signs of warmth.

BENJAMIN DISRAELI ON ROBERT PEEL

Proper old-fashioned storybook heroes require great tales of derring-do – usually with a high sea or two thrown in for good measure. In which case look no further than **Grace Darling**, the lighthouse-keeper's daughter from Bamburgh, Northumberland, who, with her father William, rowed across the stormiest and most treacherous of waters to rescue survivors from the wreck of the paddle steamship *Forfarshire* in 1838. Her heroic deed earned her not only tributes, but also marriage proposals, gifts and a £50 reward from Queen Victoria.

I have left behind the dissembling, overblown, grubby, stuck-up South and arrived back where I belong; where it's clean, spiky, tough, straightforward, unpretentious and beautiful.

JENNI MURRAY

SOMETHING TO REMEMBER US BY

THE NORTH'S CULTURAL HIGHLIGHTS

A second mention is surely merited for the world's longest-running soap opera still in production. ***Corrie*** (as it's known to its fans – thespians prefer 'The Street') is not just a national institution: it's exported worldwide to more than 40 countries as far afield as Canada, New Zealand, South Africa and Taiwan. The new set (in use from 2014) includes 54,000 cobbles and, according to facts and figures released to celebrate the soap's fiftieth birthday in 2010, the Rovers Return serves 1,440 pints a week. But only 100 G&Ts.

The wife's run off with
the bloke next door.
I do miss him.

LES DAWSON

Nothing says seaside culture like a stick of **Blackpool rock**, invented in Yorkshire by an ex-miner from Burnley, living in Dewsbury. Plain, boring forms of rock had been around for a while when Ben Bullock, on holiday in Blackpool, came up with the idea of adding the distinctive letters. Conveniently owning a boiled-sweet factory, he put his plans into action in 1887 – and hey presto… seaside rock. George Formby's song 'With My Little Stick of Blackpool Rock', recorded in 1937, was censored by the BBC's Dance Music Policy Committee – which only goes to show that some people will see innuendo anywhere.

West Yorkshire is quite dramatic and beautiful, the crags and things.

DAVID HOCKNEY

Anthony Gormley's monolithic **Angel of the North**, the celebrated rust-red sculpture standing 20 metres (66 feet) tall on a hill in Low Fell, Gateshead, has a wingspan of 54 metres (177 feet) and is made from a whopping 200 tons of steel. The position of the outstretched arms/wings led some locals to nickname it the 'Gateshead Flasher', and in 1998 a set of Newcastle United fans hoisted a giant 'Shearer 9' football shirt onto its shoulders. Gormley claimed his work, believed to be the largest angel sculpture anywhere in the world, represents 'our evolving hopes and fears'. Each year the Angel is seen by 33 million people.

One of the most successful chains in British retail culture started life as a humble market stall in Leeds' Kirkgate Market in 1884. Michael Marks' penny bazaar went from strength to strength, and in 1894 he went in search of a partner to help him grow the business further still. Enter Tom Spencer, with a £300 investment, and **M&S** was born. The first store opened in Hulme, Manchester, that same year. These days around one in four British men buy their pants from one of Marks and Spencer's UK stores (there are almost 800 to choose from). And over 124,000 people a week pick up an M&S prawn mayo sandwich.

Everything's brilliant in Leeds.

I am not an artist. I am
a man who paints.

L. S. LOWRY

Laurence Stephen (aka L. S.) Lowry, born in Stretford (then Lancashire, now Greater Manchester), is famed for his paintings of matchstick men (and cats and dogs, not to mention all manner of people in clogs) mainly in scenes in and around Pendlebury and Salford. A Manchester City fan, he turned down many awards, including an OBE, a CBE and a knighthood, and holds the record for the most rejected state honours. A bronze statue of the artist was erected in his honour in the basement of his favourite pub – Sam's Chop House – in 2011.

Multi-award-winning indie rockers the **Arctic Monkeys** from High Green, Sheffield, are just one recent addition in a long (long) line of celebrated musical acts originating in the North. They can lay claim to the honour of fastest-selling debut album in British music history, and are entirely unconnected to that other simian-themed group, The Monkees (one quarter of which was made up of Manchester-born Davy Jones). Gordon Brown was said to be a fan of the band, although, in a speech to the Labour Party Conference in 2006, he confessed he was 'more interested in the future of the Arctic Circle than the future of the Arctic Monkeys'.

There are around 3,000 consumer magazines published in the UK, but none, perhaps, can claim to have had such an impact on British popular culture as **Viz**. Born in a bedroom in Jesmond, Newcastle in 1979, *Viz* was created and edited by 19-year-old Chris Donald, with the assistance of his brother Simon and friend Jim, although most of the characters were created by Simon Thorp and Graham Dury. Famed for its irreverence, satire and bad language, at its peak *Viz* sold over a million copies and, more recently, has been exhibited in the Tate.

'I unhesitatingly gave Durham my vote for best cathedral on planet Earth,' said Bill Bryson in *Notes from a Small Island*. **Durham Cathedral** is no stranger to accolades: architectural historian Dan Cruickshank featured it in the TV series *Britain's Best Buildings* and UNESCO awarded it World Heritage status in 1986. Fans of the *Harry Potter* films will recognise it as Hogwarts School of Witchcraft and Wizardry, although a spire was added (digitally) to the towers to make it look less like a cathedral and more like a seat of supernatural learning.

I would have died for Yorkshire. I suppose once or twice I almost did.

BRIAN CLOSE ON HIS CRICKETING CAREER

Dubbed the most famous club in the world in the 1990s, Manchester's **Hacienda** may now have gone, but it will never be forgotten. Central to the 'Madchester' music scene and the rise of acid house and rave, it was founded and run by Factory Records boss Anthony 'Tony' Wilson, together with his flagship band, New Order, and their manager. The (unlikely) compère on its opening night was fellow Mancunian Bernard Manning, whose jokes went down like a lead balloon. After commenting, 'I've played some shitholes in my time, but this beats the lot,' he waived his fee and went home.

We do things differently here.

TONY WILSON ON MANCHESTER

A bit of a bad guy, certainly, but without Guido Fawkes, one of the best-loved events in the British cultural calendar would never have existed. Without Fawkes, born and bred in York, there would have been no failed Gunpowder Plot in 1605. Without Fawkes, no reason to commemorate the King's safe escape with fires – and later fireworks and burning effigies – every 5th of November. Yes – it's all thanks to Guido/Guy, good old northern Guy, we get **bonfire night** – and the perfect excuse to wave sparklers while eating toffee apples.

A desperate disease requires a dangerous remedy.

GUY FAWKES

STARS IN OUR EYES

OUR EYES

THE ENTERTAINERS WE LOVE

Eric and Ernie are not the only celebrated double act the North has to offer. Indeed Anthony McPartlin (the one who always stands on the left) and Declan Donnelly (the one who always stands on the right) have even been described in *The Telegraph* as 'the new Morecambe and Wise'. Better known as **Ant and Dec**, they've gone from children's drama *Byker Grove* via a short pop career as PJ and Duncan (with 'Let's Get Ready to Rhumble' in 1994 – and yes, they did spell 'rhumble' with an 'H') to fronting half the prime-time entertainment shows on the telly.

It was on holiday in Blackpool that Harry Corbett (nephew of Harry Ramsden of chip shop fame) bought a yellow bear glove puppet costing 7s 6d to entertain his children. Back home in Bradford, Harry dusted the bear's ears and nose with soot so they'd show up better on black and white TV, won a BBC talent show – and the rest, as they say, is history. **Sooty** and Harry became stars of the small screen and were joined by a cast of other furry friends including Sweep the dog and Soo the ~~love interest~~ panda. Famous fans include Iron Maiden's Nicko McBrain, who not only guested on *The Sooty Show*, but also features Sooty on his drum kit.

The higher the hair, the closer to heaven.

CHERYL COLE

Another talent-show winner (although this time not manufactured from man-made fibre), **Victoria Wood** – from Prestwich, Manchester – won *New Faces* in 1974 and established herself as a playwright, comedian, writer, performer and actor of note. Which is quite a lot of things to be famous for. She's probably best known for her partnership with Julie Walters, *Acorn Antiques*, *Dinner Ladies* and the much-loved 'The Ballad of Barry and Freda (Let's Do It)', which offered new possibilities of things you can do with a *Woman's Weekly*.

It gives you a great accent and, in Lancashire in particular, there's a great attitude, a refusal to be impressed.

VICTORIA WOOD ON BEING NORTHERN

Probably the most hirsute double act on British telly, ***The Hairy Bikers*** (aka Si King and Dave Myers) met in 1995 on the set of a Catherine Cookson television drama. These days King, from Kibblesworth, Tyne and Wear, and Myers, born and bred in Barrow-in-Furness, Cumbria (who, ironically, suffered from alopecia as a child) are famed not only for their hit TV shows but also their bestselling cookbooks; in 2012 *50 Shades of Grey* was knocked off the number-one slot by *The Hairy Dieters: How to Love Food and Lose Weight*. Seems the nation prefers a different kind of sauce.

They're the bestselling band in history. Winners of seven Grammys, an Oscar and 15 Ivor Novellos. They've sold 22.1 million singles in the UK alone (more than anyone else, ever) and a billion albums worldwide. Small wonder it's almost impossible to talk about **The Beatles** without a superlative (or two) thrown in. Formed in Liverpool in 1960, John Lennon, Paul McCartney, George Harrison and Ringo Starr were the ultimate boy band and, in 2004, were named 'Best Artist of All Time' by *Rolling Stone* magazine. Tributes to the Fab Four include life-size topiary figures erected on a traffic island by South Parkway Station, Liverpool, in 2008.

Liverpool people are famous for liking clothes and fashion; they are very social and lovely people and we know that they like clothes.

VIVIENNE WESTWOOD

Friends with the Beatles, signed by their manager Brian Epstein and introduced to avocados by George Harrison, fellow Scouser **Cilla Black** once worked as a coat-check girl at the Cavern Club before finding stardom on stage, screen and vinyl. She was born Priscilla Maria Veronica White in 1943: the stage name came about as the result of an error in the *Mersey Beat* newspaper that she liked and decided to keep. As well as two successive number-one singles and a gazillion series of ITV hits *Surprise Surprise* and *Blind Date*, more recently she turned down the opportunity to be a judge on the *X Factor* because she didn't want to have to put people down.

He's reputed to be Britain's nicest man and he's had two trains named after him – although he's phobic about the toilets on Virgin's Pendolinos because he doesn't trust the locking mechanism. Born in Broomhill, Sheffield, in 1943, **Michael Palin** began his entertainment career aged five, playing Martha Cratchit in *A Christmas Carol* (he fell off the stage). Comedy writer, actor and funny man, he's best known for his part in *Monty Python's Flying Circus* and as the presenter of travel documentaries that have taken him to every corner of the globe (except Middlesbrough).

The bastion of daytime telly for over 20 years, Richard Madeley and Judy Finnigan – aka **Richard and Judy** – met in Manchester, married in Manchester and lived in Manchester while presenting *This Morning* from Liverpool… on which basis it seems only fair to forgive Richard for being born down south. Ever protective of his missus, Richard once rang Judy to warn her not to open any packages after reading about a spate of parcel bombs being sent to celebs. So, when a padded envelope plopped onto the doormat, she called the police… only to discover the 'explosive' was actually a new tie for Richard from designer Jeff Banks.

You wouldn't necessarily expect to find the words 'physicist' and 'entertainer' in the same sentence. But every rule has an exception, in this case in the form of pop star turned boffin turned TV presenter **Brian Cox** (also known by some of his more, um, ardent, fans as Prof. Cox the Fox). Oldham's most celebrated scientist played keyboards for D:Ream before turning his back on pop for particles, protons and the like. Despite finding fame as an academic, he has revealed there were blips along the way: in his maths A level he only managed to scrape a D.

We explore because we are curious, not because we wish to develop grand views of reality or better widgets.

BRIAN COX

I've never really had a desire to do Shakespeare. For me, it's just too many lines.

DANIEL CRAIG

The name's Craig. **Daniel Craig**... 007 since 2005. Craig, the only James Bond to have been born after the series of films began, is one of Cheshire's own. The fact he didn't fit the tall, dark stereotype of your average Bond (what with being blond and only 5ft10in) caused something of a stir, but Roger Moore rated him the best Bond ever. Craig has suffered for his art – while filming *The Quantum of Solace* he managed to slice the top off one of his fingers – but, on a happier note, has been dubbed 'one of the best kissers' in show business by Angelina Jolie.

I'm a believer in safe sex. I put a handrail around the bed.

KEN DODD

THE WRITE STUFF

STUFF

FAMOUS WRITERS, POETS
AND PLAYWRIGHTS

The Prelude is considered to be his greatest work, but for most of us nothing says **William Wordsworth** more than 'I Wandered Lonely as a Cloud'. First published in 1807, it's Wordsworth's revised version of 1815 (where, among other small changes, 'dancing' daffodils became 'golden' daffodils) that has become one of the nation's best-known and best-loved verses of all time. Two hundred years after the poet penned those famous lines they were immortalised on video… by a rapping red squirrel, courtesy of Cumbria Tourism who wanted to 'keep it alive for another 200 years' by engaging 'the YouTube generation'.

Fill your paper with the breathings of your heart.

WILLIAM WORDSWORTH

Another writer to set his most celebrated works in the Lake District is **Arthur Mitchell Ransome**. Ransome was born in Leeds in 1884 and began his career as a foreign correspondent, covering World War One and then the Russian Revolution, where he got to know leaders including Lenin and Trotsky. After further adventures in Eastern Europe and a slight run-in with MI5, Ransome settled in the Lakes, where he wrote the first books in his hugely successful *Swallows and Amazons* series. Ransome was awarded the inaugural Carnegie Medal (the UK's most prestigious award for children's writing) in 1935 and a CBE in 1953.

After struggling to find anyone to take it on, it's said that **Emily Brontë** of Haworth, Yorkshire, paid £50 to have *Wuthering Heights* published in 1847, under the pseudonym of Ellis Bell. Emily shares her birthday (30 July) with singer songwriter Kate Bush, whose debut single 'Wuthering Heights' spent weeks at number one across the globe. On another globe entirely (Mercury to be precise) you will find a 60-kilometre (37-mile) deep crater named in honour of Emily Brontë and her sisters Charlotte and Anne.

Born in Coventry, yes, but it is **Philip Larkin**'s adopted city of Hull – where he lived and worked for over 30 years – that remains synonymous with the man considered to be Britain's greatest post-war poet. It's in Hull that you will find the 'Larkin Trail', and in Hull that a bronze statue of Larkin was erected 25 years after his death. Larkin had no issue with his work being associated with gloom – in his own words, 'Deprivation is for me what daffodils were for Wordsworth.'

Having got here, it suits me in many ways. It is a little on the edge of things, I think even its natives would say that.

PHILIP LARKIN ON HULL

Manchester, the belly and guts of the nation.

GEORGE ORWELL,
THE ROAD TO WIGAN PIER

Jeremy Clarkson might not be the first name that springs to mind when you start to list the great writers of the North – but you can't argue with the facts. A list of the 'most valuable authors' since records began, published in *The Bookseller*, puts Doncaster-born Clarkson at number 24, one place behind Roald Dahl (Welsh by birth) and one ahead of Francesca Simon (American), with £41.5 million of book sales to date. Which is quite a lot. Best known for presenting *Top Gear* and courting controversy, Clarkson has written more than a dozen successful books – not all of them about cars.

Even over 100 years after publication, *Alice's Adventures in Wonderland* is, without question, one of the great classics of children's literature. Although less so in the Chinese province of Hunan where, in 1931, it was banned because the governor believed that encouraging children to regard animals and human beings on the same level was 'disastrous'. Alice was the creation of Charles Lutwidge Dodgson – better known as **Lewis Carroll** – who was born in Daresbury, Cheshire, in 1832 and worked not only as an author, but also as an artist, photographer, mathematician and clergyman.

It's hard to say whether crime writer extraordinaire **Lynda La Plante** is better known for her hugely popular television series, including *Widows* and *Prime Suspect*, or her many bestselling novels. Born Lynda Titchmarsh in Liverpool, she first found fame as an actress onstage and in series ranging from *Z-Cars* and *The Professionals* to kids' favourite *Rentaghost*, under her screen name Lynda Marchal. La Plante is the first layperson ever to be awarded an honorary fellowship by The Forensic Science Society. Apparently her favourite meal is shepherd's pie topped with (crispy) cheese.

The History Boys, *The Madness of King George III*, *Talking Heads* – to name just three of (very) many. Is it any wonder that **Alan Bennett** is widely regarded as the greatest English playwright of his generation? Born in Leeds (where he went to primary school with Barbara Taylor-Bradford), he was once described as 'England's cultural teddy bear'. In 2010 a BBC arts programme asked him the same set of questions on the television plays of Alan Bennett as a *Mastermind* contestant. The *Mastermind* contestant got more answers correct.

If you think squash is
a competitive activity,
try flower arranging.

ALAN BENNETT

Another huge seller (more than 123 million copies), prolific writer (almost 100 books) and celebrated northerner (born in South Shields), **Dame Catherine Cookson** is said to be England's most widely read novelist. Her many stories of hardship and adversity, set in North East England, were inspired by her own deprived youth in and around County Durham. For 17 consecutive years she was Britain's most borrowed author from public libraries.

It's no good saying one thing and doing another.

CATHERINE COOKSON

Born in Cleckheaton, West Yorkshire, (Charles) **Roger Hargreaves** wrote his first *Mr Men* book in 1971 after being asked by his six-year-old son what a tickle looked like. (Orange, with very long arms and a small blue hat apparently.) More than 40 other *Mr Men* books followed, along with 40-plus *Little Misses*, between them selling over 100 million copies worldwide in 20 different languages. In fact, in the first decade of the twenty-first century, Hargreaves (who died in 1988) sold more books than any other author bar J. K. Rowling and Dan Brown.

FOOD FOR THOUGHT

OUR LANDMARK DISHES

It has won widespread fame as Betty's bestselling dish in *Coronation Street*'s Rovers Return and you'll find it served as popular pub grub the length of Britain. But the origins of **Lancashire hotpot** are as Northern as its name suggests. Lamb and veg, slow cooked and topped with sliced potato, and served with red cabbage (preferably pickled). Nothing better on a cold, wet day. And we have plenty of those – as we're told far too often, it is grim up north after all.

Down south a sausage is, well, a sausage. But up north it becomes less a boring banger, more a thing of uncommon beauty. Witness the **Cumberland sausage** – charcuterie in art form. For 500 years the good folk of Cumbria have been coiling pork and herbs into sizzling spirals, which taste every bit as good as they look. Very handy if you're hungry – one sausage can be up to 50 centimetres (19.5 inches) long.

The early bird may get the worm, but it's the second mouse that gets the cheese.

JEREMY PAXMAN

We like our cheese crumbly up north –
and **Wensleydale** is the perfect example.
Perhaps we should gloss over the fact
that it wasn't invented by locals, but by
French monks who'd settled in North
Yorkshire. Instead, let us focus on the fact
that George Orwell rated it the second-
best cheese in the world (after Stilton).
And Oscar-winning Wallace and Gromit
are fans too. They now have their own
(non-animated) Wensleydale cheese, the
popularity of which has seen exports of
Wensleydale increase by 23 per cent.

When it comes to traditional Northern grub, low-carb isn't really an option. With potato and pastry as staples, many of our classics would have Dr Atkins turning in his grave. But let that take nothing away from the **Eccles cake** (also known, mainly by small boys, as 'Squashed Fly Pie'). Salford City Council describe the currant-filled flaky pastries as 'the dessert for the discerning palate'. And they are absolutely right.

Roast beef and Yorkshire pudding is my personal signature dish.

BEN ELTON

You surely can't trump a pudding that can be served with meat and gravy for main course and filled with jam or syrup for dessert – but then the **Yorkshire pudding** is a pretty tough act to beat, whichever way you look at it. It may have started as a cheap way to pad out a costly bit of beef – but it soon became a staple of Sunday lunch. Just beware inferior imposters – according to a ruling by the Royal Society of Chemistry in 2008 'a Yorkshire pudding isn't a Yorkshire pudding if it is less than four inches tall'.

We do like our batter up north – and if it's not being used to make a Yorkshire pud, you'll likely find it coating your cod down the chippie. But fish and chips would be nothing without a side of **mushy peas** – dried marrowfat peas soaked in boiling water and bicarb for at least 12 hours, then simmered with salt (and sometimes sugar) to taste – often along with a (controversial) dollop of green food colouring to produce the distinctive hue. Perhaps best not to think about that bit.

I thought coq au vin
was love in a lorry.

VICTORIA WOOD

For those who prefer their legumes a little less lurid the answer may be **pease porridge** (aka **pease pudding**) – hot or cold but possibly not, in these days of advanced food hygiene, in the pot nine days old. Made from split yellow peas boiled in stock, it's traditionally served with salty foods, such as gammon or boiled bacon, and is possibly one reason why it gets so windy up on them there hills.

If you like to eat your chips in a **butty** (a nineteenth-century abbreviation for buttered bread, aka Northern speak for a sandwich) then you'd do well to stick them in a **barm** – a soft flat cake of bread that's traditional in Lancashire and the north-west, and just the thing for a pile of fried potatoes and a dollop of ketchup. Though if you're really hungry you may want to head further east to grab a **stottie** – the barm's bigger and heavier cousin.

There was a massive poster of me down my road, right outside the chip shop. I was about to go in, but then I saw it and changed my mind.

JESSICA ENNIS-HILL

Legend has it that **Kendal Mint Cake** (not technically a cake, given it's mainly sugar, glucose and peppermint with not a whiff of flour, eggs or butter) came about from a batch of glacier mints gone wrong. But that's not stopped it from becoming a firm favourite, especially with climbers and walkers. Sir Edmund Hillary even enjoyed a bar sitting on top of Mount Everest after his successful ascent in 1953. High praise indeed. (About 8,848 metres/29,000 feet high to be precise.)

What would Bonfire Night be without a slice of **parkin** – the cake that should NEVER be eaten fresh but instead left to mature into an irresistibly moist stickiness. Both Lancashire and Yorkshire claim parkin as their own (cue War of the Roses II – the cake-tin version) and the recipes vary accordingly. Either way ginger, spice, oats and treacle are generally essentials.

MAPPING THE NORTH

OUR WEATHER AND GEOGRAPHY

A recent survey found **the most romantic place** in the whole of the UK… is the Lake District. Not, perhaps, a shock when you consider that it boasts 2,292 square kilometres (885 square miles) of outstanding natural beauty and attracts over 15 million visitors a year. One famous tourist to be seduced by the splendour and romance of England's largest National Park was former US President Bill Clinton, who proposed to Hillary on the banks of Ennerdale Water in 1973. She said no – and made him wait another two years. Although she did agree that the setting was 'beautiful', which is the main thing.

The Lake District is also home to **England's largest natural lake**, Windermere, which is 17 kilometres long (10.5 miles; or 1,459 hectares for those keen on establishing square footage). Formed in a glacial trough, the lake has frozen solid several times, once (in 1895) for as long as six weeks. Several world water-speed records have been set on Windermere… which is also rumoured to contain a monster, affectionately known as Bownessie.

A sort of national property, in which every man has a right and an interest who has an eye to perceive and a heart to enjoy.

WILLIAM WORDSWORTH ON THE LAKE DISTRICT

Still in the Lakes… Scafell Pike (not to be confused with the peak named Sca Fell, with a height of 964 metres/3,163 feet, right next to it) stands at 978 metres (3,208 feet) and is **the highest point in England**. Until the early nineteenth century, many believed nearby Helvellyn to be the tallest mountain in the land – but then someone decided to measure them and the pike peaked 14 metres (46 feet) higher. **The deepest lake in England** – Wastwater at 79 metres (259 feet) – lies at its foot.

Statistics from the Met office show Preston is **the rainiest city in England** with an average of 103.36 centimetres (41 inches) of rainfall a year (narrowly trumping Huddersfield with a slightly less soggy 102.84 centimetres/40.5 inches). For those averse to a downpour, rest assured Preston has much, much more to offer than prize-winning precipitation. Europe's largest bus station for starters. And the UK's biggest halal meat supplier. Not to mention Deepdale Stadium – said to be the oldest professional footballing site in the world.

You know the four seasons
– winter, still winter, not
winter and almost winter.

NORTHERN JOKE

Statistics also show that we can claim **the coldest place in England** too. Cross Fell, the highest point in the Pennines at 893 metres (2,930 feet), can be covered in snow for up to 140 days a year, sometimes as late as June or July. It's gusty (understatement) up there too: the Helm Wind – the only named wind in all of the UK – is famously fierce and, in the reign of William the Conqueror, is rumoured to have blown an entire French cavalry off its horses.

The Humber bridge, leading from Hessle in the East Riding of Yorkshire to Barton-upon-Humber in North Lincolnshire, is **the longest single-span suspension bridge** in the North – in fact in all of the UK – and the seventh longest in the world. Officially opened by the Queen in July 1981, it took nine years to build and has a central span of 1,410 metres (4,640 feet). It's also the longest single-span suspension bridge ANYWHERE on the planet that you can cross on foot or by bicycle.

It's nice up north.

**GRAHAM FELLOWS AKA
JOHN SHUTTLEWORTH**

It's not so much grim up north as green. And if you're a fan of foliage you'd do well to visit Sheffield, which has a **higher ratio of trees to people** than any other city in Europe: with a population of about 550,000 and approximately two million trees it works out around 4:1. Over in the more industrial part of town – which is where Liquorice Allsorts were invented – they manufacture more than half the surgical blades used worldwide. Sheffield also boasts Europe's largest outdoor artificial ski resort.

Nothing says tradition like a maypole – and **the tallest maypole in England** (all 26.2 metres/86 feet of it) can be found in Barwick-in-Elmet, Leeds. In a ritual that takes place every three years, this impressive landmark is lowered on Easter Monday, spruced up a bit, then put back up – with much pomp and ceremony – on Spring Bank Holiday Monday. The Barwick Maypole (or at least bits of it – it's not so easy to hide 26 metres of Scots pine) has been stolen three times to date.

Manchester has everything except a beach.

IAN BROWN

The highest pub in England, indeed Britain, is the Tan Hill Inn in Swaledale, North Yorkshire. Perched at 528 metres (1,732 feet) above sea level, it dates back to the seventeenth century and starred – alongside Kyle MacLachlan – in the first Vodafone advert (in the 1990s) as well as two advertising campaigns for Everest Windows. The most popular ale served at Tan Hill is 'Ewe Juice': brewed on the premises it's named for the lambs that like to urinate around the bar (although, the owner is keen to point out, this 'does get washed up in seconds').

London has Trafalgar Square. Northern Europe, Alaska and Canada can claim the Arctic Circle. But only West Yorkshire can boast a **Rhubarb Triangle**. Less mysterious and rather more productive than its Bermuda namesake, it covers 23 square (triangular?) kilometres (9 square miles) and stretches between Wakefield, Leeds and Bradford. Rhubarb is native to Siberia, so cold, wet northern winters are ideal for producing the perfect crop. In 2010 Yorkshire forced rhubarb was granted Protected Designation of Origin status by the European Union.

THE

OBJECTS OF

OUR DESIRE

ICONIC OBJECTS AND
FAMOUS INVENTIONS

The nineteenth century saw many an inventor experimenting with the concept of electric light – but it was the filament fiddling of Sunderland's Sir Joseph Wilson Swan that finally resulted in the incandescent **light bulb** in 1878 (pipping Thomas Edison to the post). Cue many world firsts: Swan's home, in Gateshead, the first to have electric light; Mosely Street, in Newcastle, the first public road lit by electricity; and Cragside, Northumberland, the first private residence to use hydro-electricity.

Described in the House of Commons as 'the most brilliant invention ever produced in the interests of road safety', the **catseye** was the brainchild of Percy Shaw from Halifax. Driving home down a winding hill one dark night, he was saved from veering off the edge of the road by a reflection which, on closer inspection, he realised came from the eyes of a (handily) meandering moggy. In 1935, after perfecting the design, Shaw founded Reflecting Roadstuds Ltd and catseyes went into mass production. On UK roads alone there are currently estimated to be over 500 million in use.

Fans of **fizzy water** may not be aware that it's a northerner, one Joseph Priestley of Birstall, near Batley, Yorkshire, that we have to thank for the bubbles. Back in 1767, Priestley, a clergyman and chemist, worked out that by getting carbon dioxide to dissolve into water – a process he described as 'impregnating water with fixed air' – he could create a refreshingly sparkling drink. Those with a propensity for making mistakes in pencil may also like to know that another of Priestley's inventions was the rubber.

What do yer want to go to London for? It's nowt but 20 Doncasters laid end to end.

LESLEY GARRETT'S FATHER TO HIS DAUGHTER

While rudimentary versions had appeared as early as the nineteenth century, the **crossword** as we know it, was invented in 1913 in America… by a northerner. Arthur Wynne of Liverpool originally dubbed his puzzle the 'Word-Cross' – 'crossword' came from a typesetting error in the *New York World* some weeks later. The first clue set by Wynne was (at two across in case you were wondering) 'What bargain hunters enjoy'. Answer – sales.

They say necessity is the mother of invention… so perhaps it's no great shock that the creator of the **windscreen wiper** hails from the North (Whitley Bay to be precise). Or at least, that is, one of the creators, as there seem to be a number of claims as to who actually came up with the idea first. In this instance, Newcastle United's official photographer Gladstone Adams drove back from the 1908 FA Cup Final at Crystal Palace (where his team lost 3–1 to Wolves) and got fed up with having to clear snow from his windscreen by hand en route. His design for the 'moving squeegee' was patented in 1911.

Where there's muck
there's brass.

NORTHERN SAYING

It may now be named after him, but Joseph-Ignace Guillotin shouldn't claim all the credit for the famous head-chopping-off device. In fact several hundred years before the **guillotine** era of the French Revolution, a similar machine – known as 'The Halifax Gibbet' – was doing a pretty good job of beheading ne'er-do-wells in West Yorkshire. The Gibbet was banned in 1650 when Oliver Cromwell decided capital punishment was a bit over the top for a spot of petty thieving.

There are fruit drinks and then there are fruit drinks. **Vimto**, the pick of the crop for any self-respecting northerner, was invented in 1908 by wholesaler (John) Noel Nichols of Blackburn. Originally christened Vim Tonic (shortened to Vimto four years later), it was indeed sold first as a health tonic rather than a cordial. Its popularity reaches way beyond the North – it's reported that, for over 80 years, Vimto's been the most popular drink in many Arab countries for breaking the sunrise-to-sunset fast during the month of Ramadan.

I feel close to the rebelliousness and vigour of the youth here.

ERIC CANTONA ON MANCHESTER

It's true that the phrase **'Direct Drive System'** might not mean much to most of us, but as innovations go it's a good one (at least it is if you've a penchant for a 99). And a clever system it is too, in this case allowing ice-cream van engines to power soft ice-cream machines. Bryan Whitby, founder of Whitby Morrison of Crewe in 1962, helped pioneer the system, which is still in use today. Crewe is now recognised as the global home of ice-cream vans – it's estimated that around 90 per cent of the world's soft ice-cream vans have been made there.

The most glamorous invention ever?
Perhaps not. But let us take nothing
away from Sir John Charnley, pioneer
of the modern **hip replacement** and
to whom, every year, 35,000 patients in
England and Wales (on the NHS alone)
are supremely grateful. Charnley, who
was born in Bury, Lancashire, and studied
medicine at Manchester University, was
so dedicated to his craft that he even
tested out potential materials in his own
leg before using them on actual patients.
The first successful full replacement took
place in Wigan in November 1962.

Here, it's found fame as a cough sweet. In Germany, it's a much-loved pick-me-up. In parts of the Far East, it's regarded as a luxury treat. Yes, it may be small, brown and a tad on the pungent side, but since 1865 the **Fisherman's Friend** has become a veritable institution in more than 100 countries worldwide. It was pharmacist James Lofthouse of Fleetwood, Lancashire, who devised a potion of menthol and eucalyptus for local fishermen to take to sea, which he then turned into a lozenge to overcome issues of large waves and spillage. Now it's big business with five billion 'Friends' sold every year.

A LAW UNTO OURSELVES

OURSELVES

STATUTES, TRADITIONS
AND SUPERSTITIONS

One oft-quoted law is that in Liverpool **it is illegal for a woman to be topless unless she is a clerk in a tropical fish store**. Despite the fact this has found its way into countless newspapers of repute, the Law Commission has cast doubt on whether it ever truly existed as a legal statute. Nonetheless, for the avoidance of doubt it might be as well to remain fully clothed in public when visiting Merseyside.

There's nowt so queer as folk.

NORTHERN SAYING

Visitors from north of the border, especially those with a fondness for archery, may be pleased to know that it is no longer **legal to murder a Scotsman within the ancient city walls of York if he is carrying a bow and arrow**. Likewise, Welshmen within the city walls of Chester after midnight no longer need worry about someone taking a perfectly legitimate pop at them. These days modern criminal law (quite rightly) looks askance at anyone with murderous intent, whichever city walls they happen to be within.

Less a law, more a maxim, but the oft-quoted **'Marry in haste, repent at leisure'** has its origins based firmly in Yorkshire. It was penned in 1693 (in the play *The Old Batchelour*) by one William Congreve, whose other gems included a line from *The Mourning Bride* more famously shortened to 'Hell hath no fury like a woman scorned'. Congreve was born in Bardsey, Leeds, and never actually married, in haste or otherwise.

Never trust a man who wears ankle socks.

JARVIS COCKER

Putting shoes on a table has long been considered unlucky and a number of theories abound as to why. Some say it dates back to the days when criminals were hanged with their boots on. Others cite hygiene (which we'd all agree is quite fair enough). But the most commonly-held hypothesis concerns the collieries of northern England: if a miner was killed, his boots were returned and placed on the table as a mark of respect. Other mining superstitions include the fact that it is bad luck to enter the pit if you meet a redheaded woman en route.

We love a jolly northern tradition – and surely there is none jollier than the **Bacup Nutters Dance**? Every Easter Sunday, the Nutters – or to give them their full title, the Britannia Coco-Nut Dancers – tie wooden 'nuts' made from bobbins to their knees, wrists and waists and, in a ritual described by A. A. Gill as 'bizarrely compelling', dance 11 kilometres (7 miles) across the small town that lies midway between Rochdale and Burnley. The dances (and fancy costumes) are rumoured to have originated from Moorish pirates and were brought to Lancashire by Cornish miners.

As you get older three things happen. The first is your memory goes, and I can't remember the other two...

NORMAN WISDOM

An alternative annual Easter institution is the **World Coal Carrying Championship**, which takes place in Gawsthorpe, West Yorkshire. An endurance test that involves carrying a sack of coal – obviously – over a 1-kilometre (0.8-mile) distance, the tradition dates back to the 1960s and started as a bright idea over a pint. Children carry sacks weighing 10 kilogrammes (1.5 stone), women 20 kilogrammes (3 stone). Men have to lug a whopping 50 kilogrammes (almost 8 stone) around the course, so no big surprise that most of the winners have been window cleaners, farmers and builders.

Another brainwave that started life down the pub – this time over Sunday lunch – is the **Yorkshire Pudding Boat Race** held in Brawby, North Yorkshire. Artist Simon Thackray looked over at the plates of roast beef with traditional accompaniments… and pondered over what it would be like to sail, rather than eat, a giant Yorkshire pud. He tried out a prototype in the bath – and the first race was held in 1999. Coated in boat varnish to stop them disintegrating mid-competition, the traditionally made puddings – each requiring 50 eggs – are paddled using (non-edible) oars.

Further west, in Cheshire, there's always a good time to be had at the **World Worm Charming Championships**, held in Willaston near Nantwich. So popular is the contest (established in 1980), that a regulatory body, the International Federation of Charming Worms and Allied Pastimes (aka IFCWAP), was set up to ensure fair play. The most reliable method of (legally) enticing the grubs from the ground is, apparently, 'twanging' (vibrating the turf with a garden fork) – and the world record currently stands at 567 worms in 30 minutes.

There's a heart to northern style – there's no guile, no side, only great spangly fake-tanned joy.

LAURA BARTON

It's not pretty, but it's very definitely Northern and Cumbria is, without doubt, the epicentre of the gurning community. Indeed, the **World Gurning Championships** are held there in Egremont and it's a local man – one Tommy Mattinson – who holds the world record for the most wins (12 and counting). Gurning traditionally requires one to sport a horse collar while distorting the face as much as is humanly possible. Dentures may be removed or left in situ while competing, although a lack of teeth can prove to be a great advantage.

Cumbria also plays host to the **World's Biggest Liar Competition** – held for over a century in honour of Will Ritson, landlord of the Bridge Inn, Santon Bridge, who was famed for telling tall tales to entice his customers into staying (and supping) longer. Rules are simple: competitors (who come from as far afield as New Zealand and South Africa) have 5 minutes to tell the tallest tale they can. And politicians and lawyers are barred from entering for being 'too skilled'.

THERE'S
NO PLACE
LIKE HOME

FAMOUS PLACES TO SEE
AND THINGS TO DO

The North can claim many great tourist attractions – among them the oldest in all of England. In 1630 Charles Slingsby of Knaresborough, North Yorkshire, fenced off **Mother Shipton's Cave** and hey presto, one tourist site that had the day trippers flocking. Ursula Sontheil (aka Mother, or Mistress, Shipton) was raised in said cave and became the nation's most famous prophetess: her predictions included the Great Fire of London and the defeat of the Spanish Armada. Alongside the cave is a 'magic' petrifying well where the high mineral content of the waters can turn pretty much anything to stone.

Britain's top theme park, attracting over five million visitors a year, can be found on Lancashire's Fylde coast. The legendary **Blackpool Pleasure Beach** was founded in 1896 and is home to the UK's tallest rollercoaster, The Big One – a stomach-churning 71 metres (233 feet) high. For 66 days every autumn, the million-plus bulbs of the Blackpool illuminations light Blackpool's entire promenade, with the switch-on performed by a top celebrity/sportsperson/soap star/comedian and, on one occasion (in 1977), a horse, using a specially adapted pedal.

I'd rather be on Blackpool beach than Bondi beach.

LEON PRYCE ON THE 2006 LIONS' TOUR OF AUSTRALIA

York – said to be the most haunted city in Europe and thus a hotspot for any self-respecting ghost hunter – is altogether awash with sites of special interest. There's the historic Minster, the largest gothic cathedral in Northern Europe. There's the National Railway Museum, the largest in the world and home to the only Bullet train to be found outside Japan. You can be privy (sorry) to all sorts of fascinating facts and figures on the Historic Toilet Tour. Or stay the night at the oldest working convent in England whose fry-ups are said to be second to nun. OK, OK…

Tourism is thirsty work – and if you're in need of a nice cup of tea then the best place to go is undoubtedly **Bettys Café Tea Rooms** of Harrogate. Bettys (whose apostrophe disappeared about 50 years ago, causing much angst to pedants everywhere) was founded in 1919 by Swiss confectioner Frederick Belmont and became an instant success. Bettys bought Taylors tea and coffee company in 1962 and these days there are six Bettys and Taylors cafés around Yorkshire, each offering 50 different teas and coffees and more than 300 types of bread, cake and other sweet treats.

With a population of just 160, the **Holy Island of Lindisfarne** lies off the north-east coast near Berwick and is known for its priory, castle and medieval religious heritage, as well as its outstanding natural beauty. The priory was founded by St Aidan in the seventh century and ransacked by Viking raiders in AD 793. The castle came later, in 1550, though Edward Lutyens did a spot of remodelling in 1901. Reached by a causeway, Holy Island is cut off by the North Sea twice a day and despite the publication of tide tables, at least one car gets stranded every month and needs rescuing by lifeboat or helicopter.

Certainly Manchester
is the most wonderful
city of modern times!

BENJAMIN DISRAELI

Beatrix Potter's former home, Hill Top, is a seventeenth-century farmhouse near Hawkshead, Cumbria, and a must-visit for any fan of Peter Rabbit. Potter bought it in 1905 with the profits from Peter – and the house, garden and surrounding countryside provided her with ample inspiration for her writing. Potter was not only an author of world-renown, but also an award-winning sheep farmer who helped to save the Lakes' native Herdwick sheep from extinction. A replica of Hill Top stands in a children's zoo in Tokyo.

It's Britain's most romantic ruin… and the place where the deadliest vampire of all time came ashore. Yes, clearly there's something for everyone at **Whitby Abbey** on the North Yorkshire coast. It provided inspiration for Bram Stoker, author of *Dracula*, in the 1890s. It's been a backdrop for many a wedding photo since, not to mention Goth festivals aplenty. And for historians, there's more than 13 centuries of, well, history ranging from Saxon kings to a World War One shelling, with the odd bloody Viking raid and Norman knight thrown in for good measure.

As the League has been won twice as many times by northern teams as southern, it seems only fitting that the **National Museum of Football** should be based in the North. Bobby Charlton is president of the 'biggest and best' football museum in the world, dubbed 'a real jewel' by FIFA President Sepp Blatter. Exhibits in this Manchester museum include the ball from the 1966 World Cup Final and the shirt worn by Maradona while being (too) ably assisted by the 'hand of God' in 1986.

East Yorkshire, to the uninitiated, just looks like a lot of little hills.

DAVID HOCKNEY

When Patrick Brontë took up the position of parson of **Haworth** in 1820, he could never have imagined that this small West Yorkshire town would one day become entirely synonymous with his family. And indeed, Haworth now boasts the Brontë Waterfall, the Brontë Memorial Chapel and Ye Olde Brontë Tea Rooms to name but three, as well as the Brontë Parsonage Museum where the famous sisters lived and wrote. Haworth is twinned with Macchu Picchu, Peru, where it was customary to use the skulls of slain enemies as drinking vessels. In Haworth it's more traditional to use a cup.

Best-known place to visit? Perhaps not.
But the huge Lovell Telescope at the
Jodrell Bank Observatory in Macclesfield,
Cheshire, is out of this world in every sense.
Built in 1957, it's followed space probes
and satellites, researched meteors and
quasars – and even been used as a secret
nuclear tracking station by the MoD. With
a diameter of 76.2 metres (250 feet), it's
the largest moveable telescope in the
UK. In *The Hitchhiker's Guide to the Galaxy*,
Jodrell Bank scientists were so busy having
a nice cup of tea that they managed
to miss the invasion of the Vogons.

If you're interested in finding out more about our books, find us on Facebook at **Summersdale Publishers** and follow us on Twitter at **@Summersdale**.

www.summersdale.com